THE
MAGNIFICENT
BOOK OF TREASURES
JAPAN

THE
MAGNIFICENT
BOOK OF TREASURES
JAPAN

ILLUSTRATED BY EUGENIA NOBATI
WRITTEN BY PETER CHRISP

weldon**owen**

Written by Peter Chrisp
Illustrated by Eugenia Nobati

weldon**owen**

Copyright © Weldon Owen International, L.P. 2024

Published by Weldon Owen Children's Books
An imprint of Weldon Owen International, L.P.
A subsidiary of Insight International, L.P.
PO Box 3088
San Rafael, CA 94912
www.insighteditions.com

Weldon Owen Children's Books:
Additional illustrations by Lisa Alderson
and Daniel Rogers
Consultant: Dr Monika Hinkel, SOAS
Designer: Karen Wilks
Cover design: Emma Randall
Editor: George Maudsley

Insight Editions:
CEO: Raoul Goff
Senior Production Manager: Greg Steffen

ISBN: 979-8-88674-057-8

Manufactured in China.
First printing, July 2024. RRD0724
10 9 8 7 6 5 4 3 2 1

FSC
www.fsc.org
MIX
Paper | Supporting
responsible forestry
FSC® C144853

INTRODUCTION

The island nation of Japan lies at the eastern edge of Asia, and is the first place to see the sun rise in the morning. From early times, Japanese emperors called their country the Land of the Rising Sun, and even claimed to be descended from the sun goddess. Protected by the sea from foreign invaders, the Japanese created a stable and lasting civilization that has enjoyed unique traditions, such as viewing the cherry blossom, that have continued for more than a thousand years.

The Magnificent Book of Treasures Japan takes you on a spectacular journey through more than 3,000 years of this beautiful culture and reveals its wonderful riches. See fierce samurai warriors with their armor and shining swords. Wonder at spectacular works of art, from a tiny carving of a demon to a giant statue of the Buddha. Find out how to play the world's oldest board game and take part in a traditional tea ceremony.

Learn about how ordinary people lived, worked, and worshipped, and look at a paper fan, a child's doll, and a wooden god. Meet a theater star and watch a tussle between mighty sumo wrestlers. Marvel at ancient bone tools, a terracotta horse, and an extraordinary painted mask.

Travel back in time to discover some of the most magnificent Japanese treasures ever made.

FACT FILE

From: Kawanishi, Hyogo

Found today: Tokyo National Museum, Tokyo, Japan

Date: 50–300 CE

Materials: Bronze

Size: 3 ft 8¾ in (1.14 m) high

CONTENTS

THE SPIRIT MASK

- This mask was carved from the wood of a cypress tree for an actor in a Noh theater play. It shows a *tengu*, a spirit-being with a long nose and red skin thought to live in the mountains and forests of Japan.

- There are around 200 types of Noh theater mask. This one is known as an *obeshimi*. An *obeshimi* has bulging gold eyes and a tightly closed mouth. The first *obeshimi* was made in the 1200s.

- Noh, which means skill, is Japan's oldest type of theater. It is slow and ceremonial, and follows strict rules. It is always performed on a bare stage with a painted backdrop of an ancient pine tree.

- In Noh theater, there are just one or two actors. They wear masks such as this one, and dance to music played by three drummers and a flute player sitting at the back of the stage. On the side, a seated group of eight people chant the story being told.

- This mask is at least 300 years old. Many Noh masks still used in plays are also very old, having been passed down through acting families. Actors treat these masks with great respect, and bow to them before they put them on. New masks are also carved today.

- Masked Noh theater performances last all day, and include five types of play.

FACT FILE

From: Edo (Tokyo)

Found today: National Gallery of Victoria, Melbourne, Australia

Date: 1600–1700 CE

Materials: Cypress wood, ground shell, red, black, and gold pigments

Size: 8¾ in (22 cm) high, 6 in (15.5 cm) wide, 4¼ in (11 cm) deep

A WARRIOR'S ARMOR

- This suit of armor was owned by a powerful samurai, a member of Japan's warrior class. From 1185, the samurai were the rulers of Japan.

- The word samurai means "one who serves." Every samurai served a great lord, or *daimyo*, who was also a general in wartime.

- The suit is made of twelve parts. Seen here are the helmet and its ornaments, a braid, the body armor, shoulder guards, and shin guards. There was also a face mask, neck guard, and skirt.

- Warriors fought on horseback and on foot using bows and swords. In battle, they moved quickly, so their armor had to be light.

- The body armor is made from hundreds of small pieces of leather and iron sewn together in rows. These allowed the samurai to bend and move easily.

- Samurai had the right to kill people they viewed as being from lower classes, such as farmers or merchants, if they felt they were not shown respect.

- The richly decorated helmet has a tall crest, the sign of the samurai's family. It allowed the warrior to be recognized on the battlefield.

- Samurai were expected to live by a code called *bushido*, the way of the warrior. Its most important values were bravery, loyalty, and self-sacrifice.

FACT FILE

From: Japan

Found today: Victoria and Albert Museum, London, UK

Date: 1400–1500 CE (body armor); 1800–1850 CE (helmet, shin guards)

Materials: Iron, lacquer, copper, deerskin, silk

Size: Approx. 5 ft (1.5 m) high

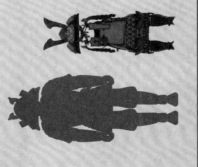

SUMO WRESTLING

- The wrestler Kawazu stands triumphant as he sends his opponent Matano thudding to the floor. This woodblock print shows the ancient Japanese sport of sumo wrestling, which is still popular today.

- The sumo wrestlers compete in a round clay ring, or *dohyo*. Each wrestler tries to push the other out of the ring or make them fall over.

- Sumo began as a religious ceremony, and the ring is still a sacred place. Before a fight, wrestlers scatter salt on the floor and stamp to drive away evil spirits.

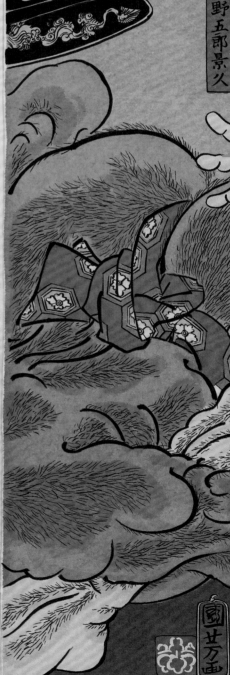

- The print is by the artist Kuniyoshi, and shows a famous match fought in 1176 between the previously undefeated Matano and Kawazu.

- On the left, the referee points a fan toward Kawazu, showing he has won.

- To the far right, future shogun Minamoto Yoritomo watches the contest from under a parasol alongside his attendants.

FACT FILE

From: Edo (Tokyo)

Found today: Private collection

Date: 1858 CE

Materials: Mulberry bark paper; ink

Size: Approx. 15 in (38.1 cm) high, 30¼ in (77.1 cm) wide

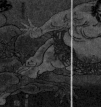

13

HORSE OF THE DEAD

- This hollow clay model, called a *haniwa*, was found at a *kofun*, or ancient tomb, where one of Japan's earliest rulers was buried.

- The terracotta figure is in the shape of a horse. It has reins, a saddle, and a harness with bells hanging from it. Japanese warriors rode horses like this into battle.

- The *kofun* at which these *haniwa* were found were built as huge mounds of earth. They were often keyhole shaped and surrounded by water. The biggest were built for the first emperors of Japan.

- Dead rulers were buried with their belongings, such as weapons, pottery, bronze mirrors, and jewelry. The Japanese believed they could use these items in the next life.

- *Haniwa* were placed around and on top of huge burial mounds rather than inside them so that they could be seen. The biggest tombs might have 15,000 *haniwa*.

- Apart from horses, there were also *haniwa* of warriors, women, houses, and ships. They may have been placed on and around tombs to guard them, or simply to show off the power of the dead ruler.

FACT FILE

From: Honshu or Kyushu

Found today: Private ownership

Date: 500–599 CE

Materials: Terracotta clay

Size: 35 in (89 cm) high, 36½ in (93 cm) long

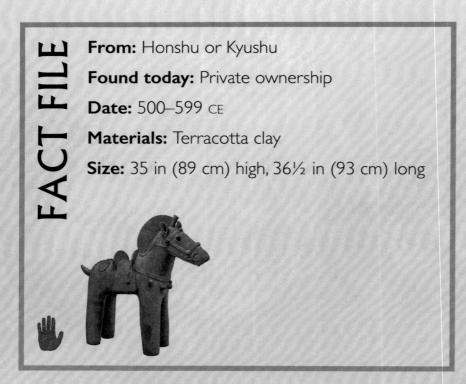

ARRIVAL OF THE PORTUGUESE

- This painted folding screen shows a type of Portuguese ship called a *nau* arriving in Japan. The Portuguese traded worldwide and in the 1500s became the first Europeans to visit Japan.

- Europeans brought with them many goods that the Japanese could not easily buy, including glassware, firearms, and Indian spices. The Japanese paid with silver and luxury goods, such as lacquerware.

- The Japanese had never seen people from Europe before. The artist has shown the Europeans with long noses, tall hats, and balloon-shaped trousers.

- The ship has just arrived, and the sailors are taking the sails up. They have tied the ship to the shore using ropes attached to the pine tree.

- Alongside the traders, the Portuguese brought missionaries. Their job was to spread Christianity. They learned Japanese, built churches, and preached. Five missionaries wearing long black robes can be seen on shore. They are welcoming the Portuguese officers to Japan.

- Folding screens had more than one use. As well as being decorative, they could be used as windbreaks in drafty Japanese homes. The Japanese word for folding screen is *byobu*, meaning "shelter from draft."

FACT FILE

From: Kyoto

Found today: Suntory Museum of Art, Tokyo, Japan

Date: 1600–1615 CE

Materials: Paper, gold leaf, ink

Size: 5 ft 5¾ in (1.67 m) high, 11 ft 8½ in (3.57 m) wide

FIGURE OF MYSTERY

- This strange-looking pottery figure is called a *dogu*, or clay figure. It was made by the Jomon people, the earliest civilization of Japan.

- More than 15,000 *dogu* have been found. There were several kinds. This type is called a *shakokidogu*, or goggle-eyed *dogu*, because of the huge, thin eyes.

- This figure was made by rolling clay into long strips. These were coiled and stacked to build up the body parts, which were stuck together using wet pieces of clay.

- The *dogu's* face and clothing are decorated with ornate dots and swirls. They were made using a pointed stick or bone.

- Most *dogu* are probably female. They usually have small waists and wide hips. Perhaps they are meant to represent goddesses.

• It is a mystery why dogu were made. They may have been used in rituals, to heal the sick, or to help women give birth.

THE CLOUD RIDER

- Lengths of cloth whip and fly about this *hiten* as it moves serenely and swiftly through the air. A *hiten*, meaning flying heaven, is a supernatural being often shown in Buddhist temple art.

- Like angels, *hiten* fly through the air acting as messengers and servants to heavenly beings. They travel by riding on clouds.

- *Hiten* are often shown singing and playing musical instruments. This one is clapping its hands.

- This is one of a group of 12 or 14 *hiten* carved on a mandorla, a decorative panel behind a giant statue of the Buddha in a temple.

- Buddhism and Shinto are the two main religions in Japan. Buddhism was often popular with Japanese people because, unlike Shinto, it offered a positive view of life after death.

- Japanese people often follow both Buddhism and Shinto at the same time. Some Buddhist temples are attached to local Shinto shrines, making it easy to practice both religions.

- The work of art this *hiten* was a part of was an image of a beautiful heavenly realm. It is where worshippers hoped to go after death.

FACT FILE

From: Joruri-ji Temple, Kizugawa

Found today: Metropolitan Museum of Art, New York City, USA

Date: About 1100 CE

Materials: Cypress wood, lacquer, gold

Size: 21 in (53.3 cm) wide

The *hiten* is about 900 years old, the same age as the Buddha statue it was made to accompany. The disk and flying sashes were later additions.

A SILKEN KIMONO

◆ Colorful flowers and bamboo fences decorate this stunning kimono. The kimono is a traditional Japanese item of clothing worn by men and women. Kimono means "thing to wear."

◆ There are several types of kimono. This one is an *uchikake*, a long, trailing robe, which is worn over a close-fitting inner kimono. *Uchikake* are mostly worn by brides at weddings.

◆ The *uchikake* is made from silk, a thin but strong thread spun by the caterpillars of a moth. People collected the silk used for this kimono and wove it into a glossy fabric called satin.

◆ Though the *uchikake*'s flower shapes and colors vary, they are all chrysanthemums.

◆ The chrysanthemum was brought to Japan from China. The Japanese loved the flower, and created hundreds of new varieties.

◆ Chrysanthemums flower in the autumn, after most other flowers. They came to represent long life, making them lucky to wear on a bride's kimono.

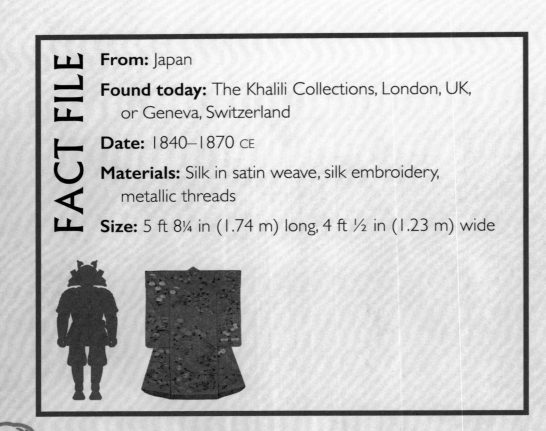

FACT FILE

From: Japan

Found today: The Khalili Collections, London, UK, or Geneva, Switzerland

Date: 1840–1870 CE

Materials: Silk in satin weave, silk embroidery, metallic threads

Size: 5 ft 8¼ in (1.74 m) long, 4 ft ½ in (1.23 m) wide

THE SILENT BELL

- This decorative bronze bell, or *dotaku*, was made by the Yayoi people, the first Japanese farmers. They came from Korea, and brought the skill of crafting bronze and iron with them.

- Bronze is made by mixing copper and tin. The Yayoi people had not yet found these metals in Japan, so they brought them from Korea and China.

- The first *dotaku* were small, and had clappers inside so they could be rung. Over time, they became bigger and no longer had clappers.

- This *dotaku* was made by pouring molten metal into molds. At first, metalworkers used stone molds carved with the patterns for a bell's surface. Later they used pottery molds, which allowed them to make bigger bells.

- Big, richly decorated *dotaku* like this one were made for display or use in harvest rituals, rather than to be rung as bells.

- This *dotaku* has zigzag lines along its sides and spirals on the decorative side ornaments. The hole near the top was for a rope so the bell could be hung up and displayed.

- *Dotaku* were found buried on hillsides, beside the fields where farmers grew their rice.

- Archaeologists have found more than 400 *dotaku* across western Japan.

- Some *dotaku* were buried on their own. Others were in collections of nearly 40. Perhaps they were buried as offerings to gods or the land to ensure a good harvest.

FACT FILE

From: Kawanishi, Hyogo

Found today: Tokyo National Museum, Tokyo, Japan

Date: 50–300 CE

Materials: Bronze

Size: 3 ft 8¾ in (1.14 m) high

THE WOODEN GOD

- Shinto is the oldest religion in Japan. It means "the way of the gods." These gods or spirits, known as *kami*, are often from nature. Mountains, lakes, rocks, trees, wind, and rain all had their own *kami*.

- Shinto shrines are seen as the homes of the *kami*. They are places of worship, where people pray to the gods and ask for their help.

- This little statue of a *kami* is from one of the most important Shinto shrines. The shrine is dedicated to Hachiman, a god of warriors and the protector of Japan.

- The dead could become *kami*. Some emperors were thought to become gods after death, and had shrines dedicated to them. Families also set up shrines in their homes to honor their ancestors, who they believe continue to watch over them.

- Statues of Shinto gods were usually made from wood. The wood was probably taken from old trees thought to be the homes of *kami*.

- The *kami* is dressed like a nobleman at court, with robes and a tall hat. He holds a *shaku*, or scepter, a sign of high office.

FACT FILE

From: Hachiman shrine, Oita, Kyushu

Found today: Metropolitan Museum of Art, New York City, USA

Date: 900–950 CE

Materials: Cypress wood, paint

Size: 20¾ in (52.4 cm) high

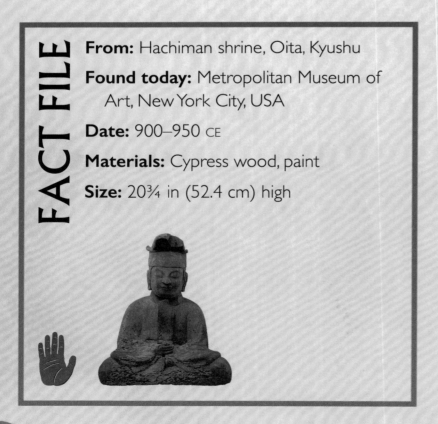

- Swordsmiths gained the knowledge of how to make the perfect sword over many years. They knew that by cooling different parts of the blade at different rates, they could make sure their swords had hard edges and soft but unbreakable cores.

- A sword's blade was polished using special stones. The polisher began with coarse stones and ended with smooth ones.

- Swords were handed down through samurai families, who often added new fittings to old blades. This sword's fittings were made 200 years after its blade.

FACT FILE

From: Osaka

Found today: Victoria and Albert Museum, London, UK

Date: 1600–1700 CE (blade); 1800–1850 CE (scabbard and fittings)

Materials: Steel (blade); lacquer, shell (scabbard); rayskin, silk, silver, gold (handle)

Size: 39¼ in (100 cm) long; blade 27½ in (70 cm) long

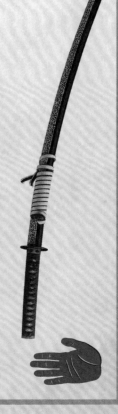

37

MIRROR OF THE GODS

- This is the richly decorated back of a bronze mirror. Its other side was smooth and would have been polished until it shone. This was so it could be used to reflect the viewer's face, just like a modern mirror.

- The mirror is a Japanese copy of a Chinese one. Around the central mound are four ornate, faded figures of Chinese gods or spirits.

- Mirrors like this were invented by the Chinese, whose emperors sent them as gifts to Japanese rulers. They were seen as magical and sacred objects by both the Chinese and Japanese.

- This mirror was found in a *kofun*, or burial mound, where it had been placed as an offering for the dead person.

- Bronze mirrors were important to the Japanese, and were a part of the imperial regalia. There was even a Shinto goddess of mirror-making called Ishikoridome.

- In Japanese myths, the sun goddess, Amaterasu, had put the world in darkness by hiding in a cave. The other gods hung a mirror outside to lure her out. On spying her reflection, she came out, bringing light back to the earth.

FACT FILE

From: Yamato (Nara)

Found today: British Museum, London, UK

Date: 300–400 CE

Materials: Bronze

Size: 8 in (20.2 cm) wide

THE LITTLE EMPRESS

- Every year on March 3, the Japanese celebrate *Hinamatsuri*, Doll's Day, also called Girls' Day. This is a festival in honor of young girls, to bring them good luck and health as they grow toward adulthood.

- Families celebrate Girls' Day by displaying little dolls, or *hina*, like this one. The *hina* are dressed in the clothing of the ancient Japanese court.

- This doll is an empress. She sits on a richly decorated base. She has a white powdered face and her clothing is patterned with birds and flowers.

- During the Doll's Day festival, dolls are displayed on platforms with several levels. An empress doll such as this one is placed on the highest level, alongside an emperor doll, showing their importance.

- Many different dolls are presented on Doll's Day. Smaller dolls are placed on the lower levels of display platforms. They represent musicians and members of the court. Little models of furniture, flowers, and cherry trees help decorate the scene.

- After the festival, the dolls are stored away rather than used as toys to be played with. It is believed that keeping them out can bring bad luck for the girls.

FACT FILE

From: Japan

Found today: Museum of Ethnography, Geneva, Switzerland

Date: 1700–99 CE

Materials: Porcelain, wood, silk, horsehair

Size: 9¾ in (25 cm) high, 13½ in (34 cm) wide, 10½ in (26.5 cm) deep

❦ Originally, the dolls' festival was celebrated only by the daughters of noble families. Today it is enjoyed by lots of different people across Japan.

❦ Boys had their own festival on May 5. Families hung colorful streamers shaped like carp fish outside their homes. In modern times, Boys' Day has been renamed Children's Day, and is for all children.

LIFE IN THE FIELDS

- Folding paper fans were invented in Japan. They were used by wealthy people to keep cool during the hot summer. But they were also beautiful works of art that were often painted with landscapes.

- This fan is so big that it might have been made for display on a wall. It is painted on both sides, and shows farmwork at different times of the year.

- This side of the fan shows autumn. The farmers have just harvested the rice crop, which they have gathered into bales.

- For centuries, rice was the most important food in Japanese diets. It is thought that rice has been farmed in the country for almost 3,000 years.

- In the distance, a loaded donkey makes its way over a hill. People raised animals for their labor rather than their meat in Japan. For many centuries, diets were mostly vegetarian.

FACT FILE

From: Edo (Tokyo)

Found today: Metropolitan Museum of Art, New York City, USA

Date: 1850–80 CE

Materials: Paper, bamboo, ivory

Size: 29½ in (75 cm) wide, 16¼ in (41 cm) high

The reverse of the fan shows the same landscape, but covered with the white snow of winter. The artist, Isei, also painted fans showing farmwork in other seasons.

A woman rests by bales of rice in the center of the fan. The painting shows us that the life of an ordinary farmer was hard. A large part of the population made their living this way for most of Japan's history.

BONE TOOLS

- This set of bone tools was made by the Jomon, the earliest Japanese culture. These people survived by hunting and gathering wild food, and lived in villages beside Japan's coasts and rivers.

- These tools were found in a rubbish dump outside a Jomon village. Over 700 years, the rubbish built up to form a mound, or midden.

- Alongside a curved fishing hook, a triangular arrowhead, and three harpoon heads is a long, thin needle. This was used to sew clothes. Jomon people made their clothes from plant fibers and animal skins.

- The rubbish dump in which these tools were found was also filled with seashells, animal and fish bones, and nutshells. These tell us that the Jomon ate a varied diet that changed with the seasons.

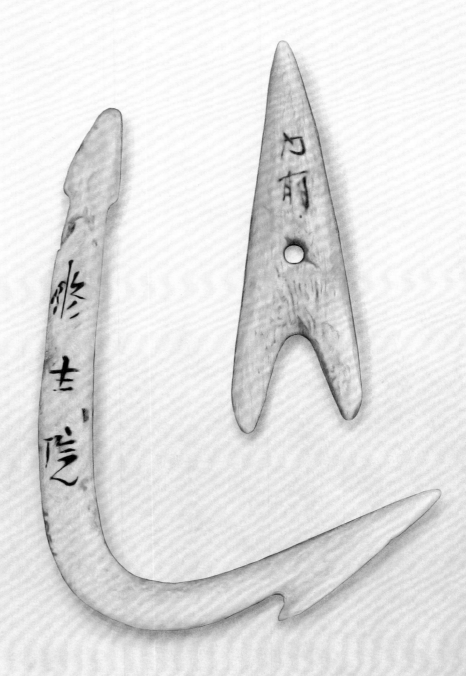

FACT FILE

From: Ofunato Bay, Iwate

Found today: Metropolitan Museum of Art, New York City, USA

Date: 1000–300 BCE

Materials: Bone

Size: Approx. 2¾–4 in (6–10 cm) long

❦ Based on the bones they threw away, it is thought the Jomon people ate more than 50 types of fish. They used nets, lines, and harpoons like these to fish mostly during the calmer spring and summer months.

❦ In autumn, the Jomon gathered nuts and fruit in the forests. In winter, they hunted deer and boar with bows and arrows, using arrowheads such as this one.

❦ Archaeologists have discovered that some Jomon rubbish mounds held boats made from hollowed-out cedar logs. These were used to hunt whales and dolphins at sea with their bone harpoons.

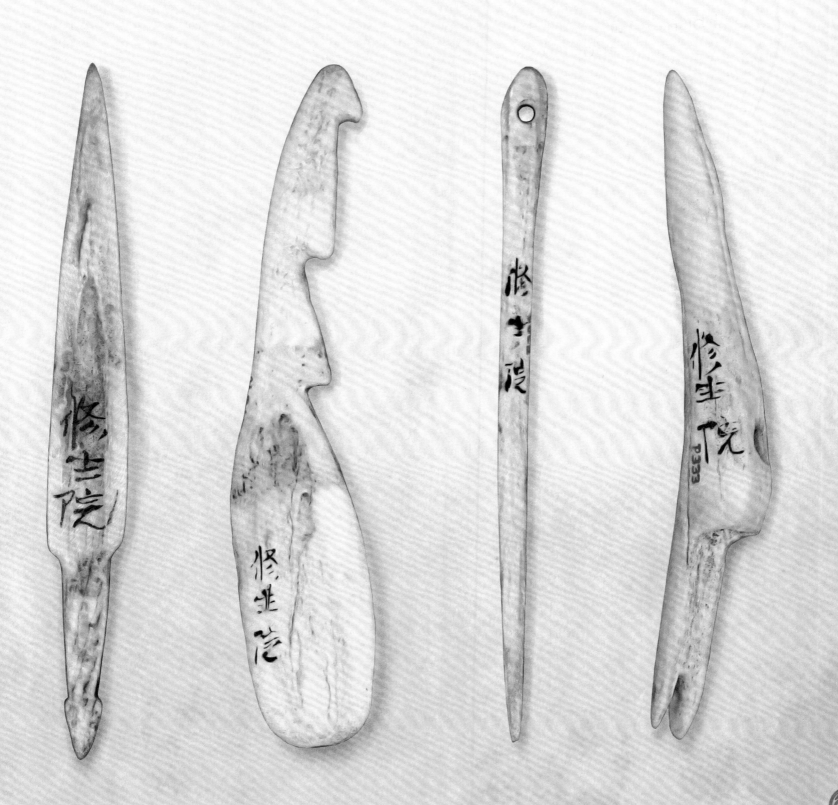

THE GREAT GENERAL

FACT FILE

From: Kyoto

Found today: Metropolitan Museum of Art, New York City, USA

Date: 1000–1185 CE

Materials: Wood, paint

Size: 13½ in (34.3 cm) high

- This seated figure is the great general, Daishogun. It was his job to defend the four cardinal directions—north, south, east, and west.

- Daishogun was a powerful guardian god in ancient Japan. Statues of the god were kept in shrines around Kyoto to stop the city from being attacked by evil spirits.

- The figure is dressed in the uniform of a Japanese general. Its right hand is clasped where it once held a sword.

- When this carving was made, diseases, earthquakes, fires, and any type of bad luck were all blamed on evil spirits. People used Daishogun figures to protect themselves from such dangers.

- This figure was made in Kyoto, the old capital of Japan, where emperors lived for more than 1,000 years. The site of Kyoto was chosen because there were mountains to the northeast and northwest, which blocked the path of evil spirits.

- The Japanese believed that evil spirits were more likely to come from particular directions of the compass. These places are where Daishogun shrines were built.

- The emperor employed people called diviners. They advised him on the best places to build palaces and temples, and shrines that might hold a Daishogun.

- The Daishogun is shown frowning. Perhaps he has just seen an evil spirit approaching.

- Traces of paint show that the figure once had a red face and wore patterned clothing beneath his armor.

MUSIC MAKER

- For centuries, the soft, soothing sounds of the koto have echoed through the courts and great buildings of Japan. This koto is protected by a lacquered case and a richly decorated silk bag.

- The sides of the koto are patterned with medallions of little gold cranes, which were the symbol of the family it was made for. The ends are decorated with gold metalwork lions and flowers.

- The instrument has 13 silk strings. They would have been raised off the wood using small bridges placed at different positions along the koto's length. Their positioning created different notes.

- Players plucked the strings using flat pieces of ivory on their thumb and the first two fingers of the right hand. With the left hand, they pushed or pulled the strings to change the sound.

- In the past, players played by kneeling or sitting on the floor, resting the koto on their knees. Modern players place it on a stand and sit on a chair.

- The koto has long been seen as Japan's national instrument.

FACT FILE

From: Kyoto

Found today: Metropolitan Museum of Art, New York City, USA

Date: 1600–30 CE (koto),
1800–25 CE (box),
1750–1850 CE (silk wrapping)

Materials: Various woods, ivory, tortoiseshell, gold, silver, silk

Size: Instrument 74½ in (189.5 cm) long, 9½ in (24.2 cm) wide

THE TEA CEREMONY

- This pot, or *suichu*, was used to carry water in a tea ceremony. The ceremony was a special way of preparing and drinking green tea.

- The Japanese tea ceremony was started by Buddhist monks, who drank tea to stay awake. The practice was later taken up by wealthy people.

- A tea ceremony was intended to allows its participants to live in the moment, to feel at peace and enjoy the beauty of nature.

- Tea ceremonies using *suichu* like this one took place in teahouses, gardens, or tearooms. These places were designed to create a sense of peace.

- The tearooms used for tea ceremonies were simply decorated. They often displayed flowers or branches in a vase, and a painted scroll showing a scene from nature might hang on a wall.

- The decoration of pots and bowls matched the changing seasons. This pot shows cherry blossoms, which appear in spring.

- During a tea ceremony, the host and their guests knelt silently on *tatami* mats, woven from rice straw and soft grass. The host made and served the tea using a series of traditional actions, from washing the utensils to measuring the tea.

FACT FILE

From: Mino, Gifu

Found today: Metropolitan Museum of Art, New York City, USA

Date: 1600–1700 CE

Materials: Clay, copper-green glaze

Size: 8¼ in (20.7 cm) high

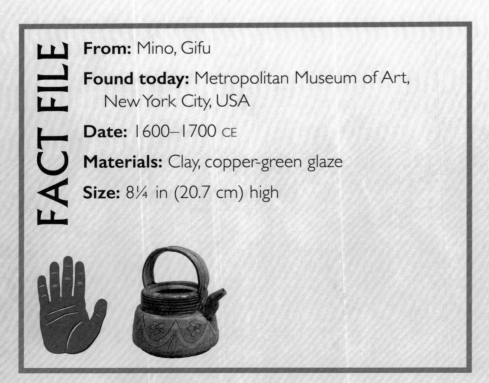

The curved shape beneath the flowers is a curtain. A curtain was used to enclose areas for picnics held among cherry trees when they were in flower.

THE HOLY MONK

- This statue is of a famous Buddhist monk and priest called Chogen, made just before the time of his death aged 85.

- Chogen is sitting cross-legged, and is holding a set of prayer beads in his hands. He uses these to count prayers.

- The statue was made for a great Buddhist temple at Todai-ji, which had been burned down during a civil war.

- The monk was very religious. He was said to have recited a prayer praising the Buddha a million times.

- Chogen spent 25 years overseeing the rebuilding of the temple of Todai-ji, as well as other temples destroyed during a civil war. He also made sure that lost works of art were replaced.

- Chogen was very persuasive. He convinced Japan's ruler and leading families to pay for new buildings, artworks, and Buddhist books.

- There was a giant Buddha statue at Todai-ji Temple. When the building was burned down, its head and left hand were lost. Chogen spent five years having the statue repaired.

- The artists and sculptors who worked for Chogen created a new style of lifelike art. The style can be seen in the look of this statue.

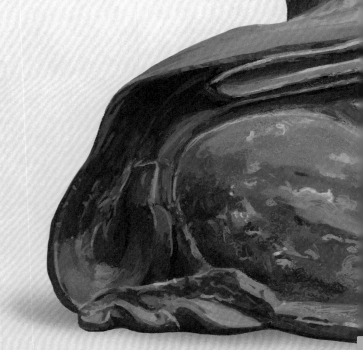

FACT FILE

From: Nara

Found today: Todai-ji Temple, Nara, Japan

Date: 1206–10 CE

Materials: Wood, paint

Size: 32¼ in (81.8 cm) high

This sculpture of Chogen shows all the signs of old age. Its neck is bent, and it has sunken eye sockets, a wrinkly neck, and shrunken cheeks.

When the paint on the statue's robe and skin was fresh, the figure would have looked just like Chogen did in real life.

NINJA ATTACK

- This print shows a warrior called a ninja sneaking up to attack a seated nobleman. Ninja means "one who is not seen."

- Unlike samurai warriors, ninjas did not follow a strict code of honor. They acted as spies and assassins, and were sent to take the lives of important people.

- Although ninjas really lived, they are best known from later stories invented about them. In art, they are dressed completely in black.

- This picture comes from a popular illustrated novel about the adventures of Prince Muuji, a handsome hero.

- Prince Muuji is shown sitting in the open air at night, playing an instrument called a koto. He glances up at a flock of geese flying in front of the full moon as the ninja approaches him.

- Although the prince seems to be wrapped up in his music, he is aware that the ninja is sneaking up behind him. We know this because the next picture in the book this print is from shows Prince Muuji pinning the ninja to the ground and seizing his sword.

FACT FILE

From: Edo (Tokyo)

Found today: Museum of Fine Arts, Boston, USA

Date: 1852–53 CE

Materials: Paper, ink

Size: 10¼ in (26.1 cm) high, 7¼ in (18.1 cm) wide

GUARDIAN OF THE SHRINES

- This snarling wooden statue is a *komainu*, a mythical animal that has a lion's head and the body of a powerful dog.

- Pairs of *komainu* were placed on either side of the entrances to Shinto shrines. One was always shown with its mouth open, like this one, while the other had its mouth closed.

- A *komainu*'s role was to act as a guard to scare away evil spirits.

- There have never been lions in Japan, but Japanese people knew what they looked like from Korean and Chinese art.

- The word *komainu* combines two Japanese words—*koma*, meaning Korean or foreign, and *inu*, meaning dog.

- The statue was once covered in gleaming gold leaf, which is now mostly worn away. The dark areas are an undercoat of black lacquer, which was painted over the wood to protect it from the rain.

- The first *komainu* were made of wood, which is easily damaged. This one has lost its tail and its rear left paw. Later, *komainu* were carved from stone or cast in bronze.

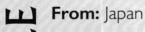

FACT FILE

From: Japan

Found today: Metropolitan Museum of Art, New York City, USA

Date: 1250–1260 CE

Materials: Cypress wood, lacquer, gold leaf, paint

Size: 18 in (45.7 cm) high

THE GREAT WAVE

- This woodblock print is the most famous and widely reproduced work in Japanese art. It was made by an artist called Hokusai.

- The print is one of a series of 36 showing unusual views of Japan's most famous mountain, Fuji. Here the mountain looks tiny in the far distance.

- The Japanese writing on the print gives the titles for the series and this picture— *Thirty-six views of Mount Fuji/On the high seas in Kanagawa/Under the wave.*

- Mount Fuji is the highest mountain in Japan. With its snow-capped top, it is seen as both beautiful and sacred.

- As the white crest of the wave breaks, it forms grasping fingers that head down toward the boats.

FACT FILE

From: Edo (Tokyo)

Found today: Art Institute of Chicago, Chicago, USA

Date: 1830–32 CE

Materials: Paper, ink

Size: 10 in (25.4 cm) high, 14¾ in (37.6 cm) wide

- The picture shows the power of nature, with the boats and fishermen helpless beneath the wave.

- In Japan, pictures are viewed from right to left. Seen this way, the wave looks even more threatening, with the boats heading straight into it.

- The blue color was made from Prussian blue, a dye invented in Germany. The color was popular with Japanese artists for its depth and long-lasting nature.

THE FIRST SHOGUN

- The powerful Minamoto Yoritomo, Japan's first shogun, or military ruler, sits quietly for his portrait. He was the head of the mighty Minamoto clan of samurai warriors.

- Yoritomo fought a five-year civil war against the rival Taira clan. After he won, he made himself the ruler of Japan.

- In the portrait, Yoritomo wears a stiff, dark robe that is richly decorated, as well as a tall cap called a *kanmuri*. In his right hand he holds a ceremonial baton. The hilt of his sword pokes out of his robe.

- Yoritomo set up a new capital at Kamakura. He called this his *bakufu*, or tent government, as if it were an army camp. This helped show off his military might.

- Japan had a long history of emperors, but the shogun claimed to rule on their behalf. The emperor continued to hold court ceremonies in his palace at Kyoto, yet had no real power.

- Japanese emperors traced their family back to Amaterasu, the sun goddess. As a result of this important connection, they could not be replaced by rulers from any other family.

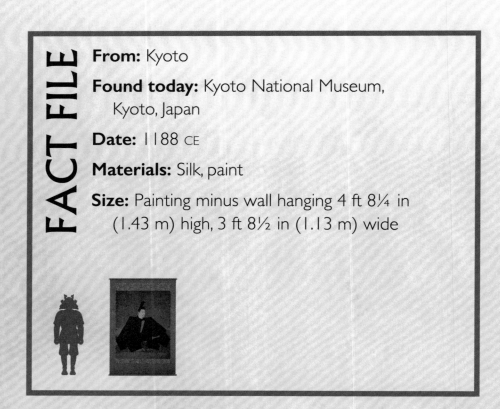

FACT FILE

From: Kyoto

Found today: Kyoto National Museum, Kyoto, Japan

Date: 1188 CE

Materials: Silk, paint

Size: Painting minus wall hanging 4 ft 8¼ in (1.43 m) high, 3 ft 8½ in (1.13 m) wide

LITTLE RED MONSTER

- This tiny carving is a *netsuke*, a toggle that was once threaded onto a cord, from which hung a wooden box worn on the sash on a man's kimono. It is in the form of an *oni*, a mythical Japanese demon.

- *Oni* were a popular subject for *netsuke*, and were often shown in comical situations. This one is in a relaxed position, although its glaring face and clawed hands and feet still give it a monstrous appearance.

- The artist carved this *netsuke* from lacquer, which comes from an *urushi* tree. The Japanese discovered that when the sticky sap of the tree dried it formed a hard, shiny, waterproof substance.

- During the spring festival of Setsubon, Japanese people throw beans out of their doors to scare away *oni* and bring good luck.

- Natural lacquer is brown, so people added minerals to color it. The red color used in this carving was made by adding cinnabar, a scarlet mineral.

- Lacquer was mostly used to varnish wooden objects, such as bowls and furniture. A big lump of lacquer could also be carved into a *netsuke*, like for this demon.

FACT FILE

From: Japan

Found today: Metropolitan Museum of Art, New York City, USA

Date: 1800–1899 CE

Materials: Red lacquer, gold paint

Size: 1¼ in (3.2 cm) high, 1½ in (3.5 cm) wide

FIREFIGHTER'S JACKET

- This colorful jacket was once worn by a firefighter in Edo, the old name for Tokyo, the capital city of Japan.

- In the 1800s, Edo was a huge city crowded with wooden buildings. Fires often broke out there, fanned by strong winds.

- Each district of Edo had its own fire brigade. Firefighters wore thick cotton jackets, or *hikeshibanten*, like this one, which they soaked in water to protect themselves from the flames.

- To stop fires spreading, firefighters would tear down the buildings surrounding the fire.

- *Hikeshibanten* were reversible. One side was plain and carried the name of the fire brigade. When fighting a fire, the fireman wore the jacket plain side out. The inside was decorated with scenes of legendary battles, in which famous samurai defeated monsters.

- After tackling a fire, a firefighter often reversed their jacket to show its decorated lining. This was a way of displaying their bravery.

- This jacket's lining shows a demon in the form of a giant spider. It has just attacked a warrior called Yorimitsu. The warrior has fought off the spider demon, which is shown retreating back into its web.

Beneath the spider on this jacket is a set for the game of Go. The story goes that the hero Yorimitsu's guards were playing this game when the spider attacked him.

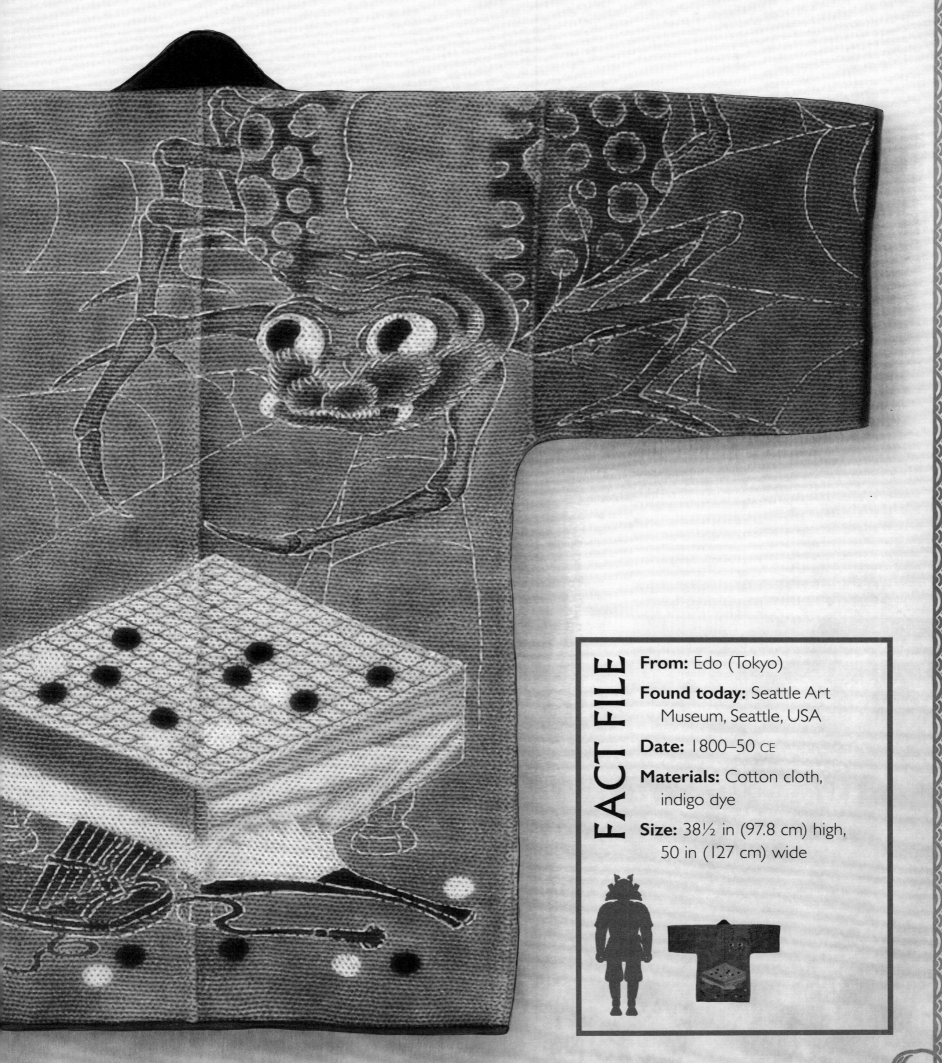

FACT FILE

From: Edo (Tokyo)

Found today: Seattle Art Museum, Seattle, USA

Date: 1800–50 CE

Materials: Cotton cloth, indigo dye

Size: 38½ in (97.8 cm) high, 50 in (127 cm) wide

THE FISH HELMET

◆ A red-masked face snarls a fierce challenge to those that behold it. It is part of a helmet worn by a high-ranking samurai warrior in the late 1500s. At the time, there was a new fashion for *kawari kabuto*, or strange helmets, which had unusual and striking designs.

◆ The iron helmet, with its accompanying face covering, is shaped like a man's head. It has red skin, a wrinkled forehead, and its hair and moustache are made of boar bristles. The fearsome face mask is set with golden teeth.

◆ On the crest of the helmet are two carp, a type of fish. They are made of wood covered with gold foil. Carp stood for strength and determination in Japan because they could swim upstream against strong currents.

◆ Helmets like this were designed to impress. Warriors going into battle wanted to be noticed by those on their own side, and feared by their enemies as strong, determined fighters who would never give up.

◆ Helmets were also worn by samurai when they were not fighting, such as during religious ceremonies and public processions. For ordinary people, the sight of a warrior wearing a magnificent helmet was a reminder that the samurai were Japan's ruling class.

FACT FILE

From: Japan

Found today: Private collection, Japan

Date: 1575–1600 CE

Material: Iron, lacquer, wood, gold foil, boar's bristles

Size: Approx. 20 in (50 cm) high

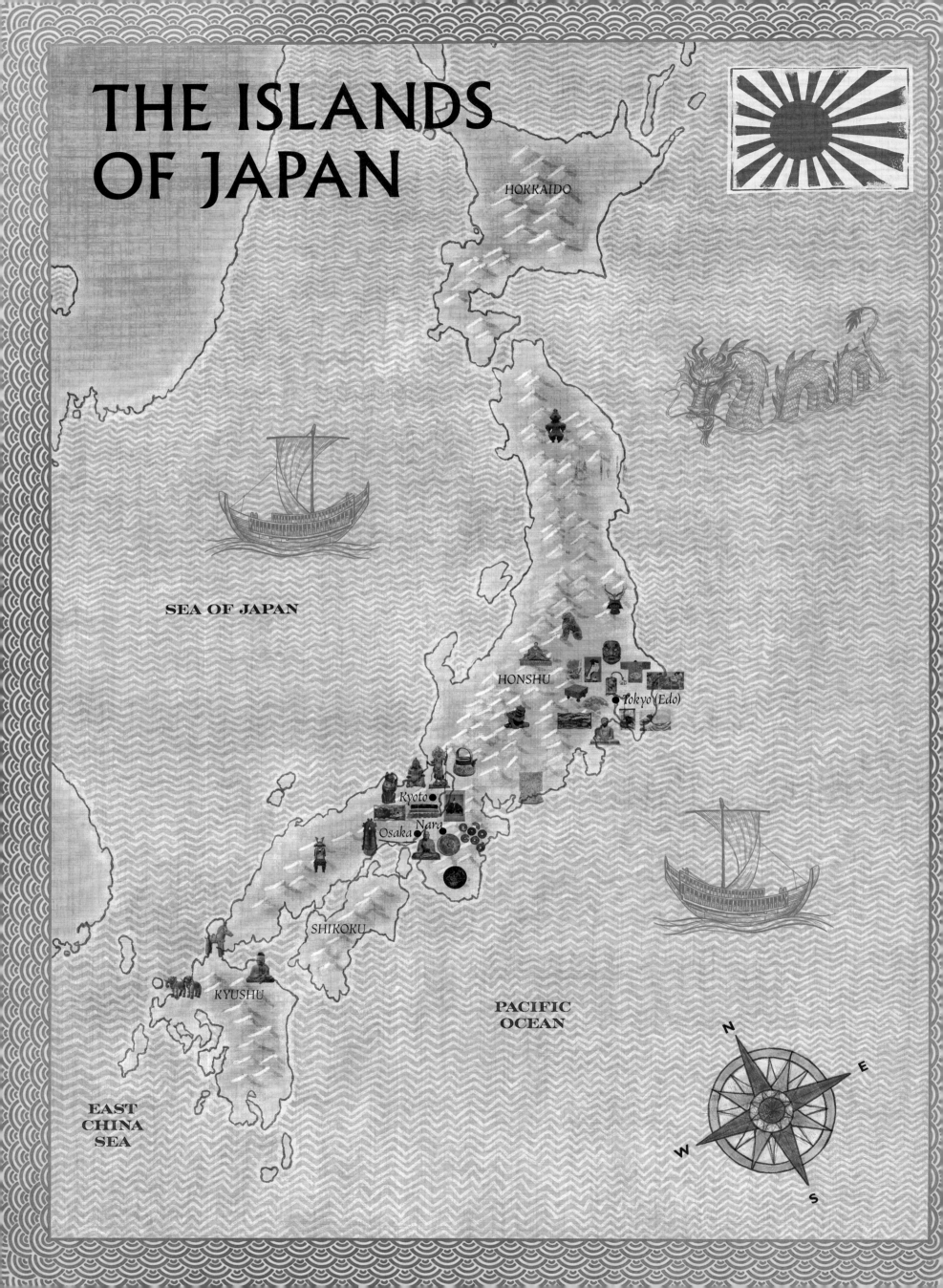

THE ISLANDS OF JAPAN

HORKAIDO

SEA OF JAPAN

HONSHU

Tokyo (Edo)

Kyoto

Osaka Nara

SHIKOKU

KYUSHU

PACIFIC
OCEAN

EAST
CHINA
SEA

N
E
W
S